A BOY CALLED BOB

Becomes an AFL Footballer

A BOY CALLED BOB

Becomes an AFL Footballer

BOB MURPHY

with Tony Wilson

PiccoloNERO

Published by Piccolo Nero,
an imprint of Schwartz Publishing Pty Ltd
Level 1, 221 Drummond Street
Carlton VIC 3053, Australia
enquiries@blackincbooks.com
www.nerobooks.com

Copyright © Bob Murphy and Tony Wilson 2019

Bob Murphy and Tony Wilson assert their rights to be known as the authors of this work.

ALL RIGHTS RESERVED.
No part of this publication may be reproduced, stored in a retrieval system, or transmitted in any form by any means electronic, mechanical, photocopying, recording or otherwise without the prior consent of the publishers.

9781760641429 (paperback)
978174380964 (ebook)

A catalogue record for this book is available from the National Library of Australia

Illustrations by Phillip Marsden
Cover design by Akiko Chan
Text design and typesetting by Akiko Chan

'To the smell of football leather

and football dreaming'

—Bob Murphy

'For every kid with a dream, and for

Peter Weightman, who coached mine'

—Tony Wilson

Contents

1

In which a nun meets a priest
and nothing is quite the same

Mum was a nun and Dad was a priest.

I'm not sure how much you know about nuns and priests, but here's the short version: THAT IS NOT HOW IT'S SUPPOSED TO WORK!

Nuns aren't supposed to go on hot dates with priests, or former priests, or even common everyday non-priests for that matter.

Priests aren't supposed to go on hot dates with nuns, or former nuns, or non-nuns.

They aren't meant to date.

They aren't meant to fall in love.

They aren't meant to have kids.

They *are* meant to dedicate themselves wholly and truly to God.

If you've seen *The Sound of Music*, you'd know that VERY OCCASIONALLY young, pretty nuns who are quite good at singing will spin around in a field for a bit, before going off and falling in love with an army captain who is looking for a good babysitter.

That's an unusual love story.

My parents' love story is unusual too.

Mum wasn't the only nun in her family. Three of her sisters were nuns. She is actually one of 14 kids, so there were plenty of non-nuns in the mix too. Mum says she never much liked the strict rules that went with being a nun.

Dad hadn't been a priest very long when he agreed to drive a carload of nuns down to the beach one Saturday afternoon. His eyes widened when Mum came out of the convent door, wearing her most beachy nun clothes, casually swinging her handbag on her index finger.

For Dad, it was love at first sight. 'From that moment, nothing was ever the same.'

Mum stopped being a nun, Dad stopped being a priest, and both of them became teachers. They married and had three kids – Ben, Bridget and me, Robert. Later known as Robbie. Much later known as Bob.

When we were kids, Ben, Brig and I were obsessed with the details of how they met. 'Hey, Mum, did you pash Dad while he was still a priest?'

But now we are in awe of their love story. They upturned their lives for each other, and, eventually, for us.

Ben and Brig were born in Alice Springs, while Mum and Dad were teaching in the Indigenous community at Yulara. Mum found out she was pregnant with me when she fainted in the shadow of Uluru.

Soon after that, the Murphys returned to Ballarat in Victoria. I was born on the

9th of June 1982 at 6 pm. The nurses wrapped me up and handed me to Dad, and I gently stroked his face with my right hand.

One day a priest met a nun, and nothing was ever the same.

2

In which Bob shares some important lessons about moving cars

I can't believe we've made it to Chapter 2 and I HAVEN'T EVEN TOLD YOU HOW TO MAKE A SOCK FOOTY YET! This is one of the most important things you can learn in childhood, up there with brushing your teeth and not jumping out of moving cars.

So here it is.

HOW TO MAKE A SOCK FOOTY

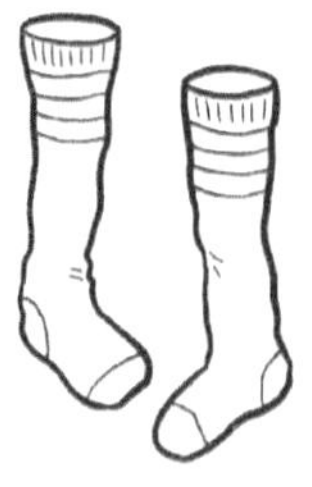

You need
thick socks —
like Explorers —
for this.

Take folded
socks.

Stuff folded
socks down.

Twist at middle.

Pull down
from top to
make footy.

Ben and I played sock footy for hours. We had a sliding door in our living room, and we'd narrow the gap a little at a time to make the shot more and more difficult. We got quite good, and only broke a dozen or so of Mum's most precious vases.

I was always wanting to play with my brother and sister. Ben is five years older than me, and Brig four, so I was the annoying little bro. In fact, they invented a game called 'S.P.I. on Robbie'.

The rules of 'S.P.I. on Robbie' are chilling, even to this day.

Here they are, in all their cruelty:

Get sick of hanging out with Robbie.

Yell 'S-P-I on Robbie!' and run away and hide.

Robbie cries.

Mum comes outside and flips out.

Laugh hysterically.

It might have been a better game if you weren't a Robbie. I hated it. I'm not sure why Ben and Brig spelled it 'S.P.I. on Robbie' when they meant 'Spy on Robbie'. Maybe it was brilliant espionage. More likely, they couldn't spell. Morons.

They generally included me in their games, even though I was the little one. Our favourites included:

Cricket: I'm a left-hander. Our backyard pitch sloped away to the left, which was great for Ben's outswinger. When I was very young, I'd really taken to heart the rule of staying in my crease.

I stubbornly believed I couldn't be out if I stayed in my crease. If my brother took a catch – 'Not out! I'm still in my crease.' If he bowled me middle stump – 'Not out! I'm still in my crease.' Of course the downside was I didn't score many runs ... I was too afraid to leave my crease.

Street footy: There was a tree in the nature strip, the perfect distance from a power pole. If the AFL had decided to make one goalpost a power pole and the other a spindly native, I would *definitely* have kicked more than 187 goals in my career. Other players may have complained, however.

Climbing Herbie: Herbie was the name we gave the six-metre-high gum tree in the front yard at 186 Albert Road, Warragal. We named it after a personality-packed VW Beetle who'd starred in a few movies. Why was this a good nickname? You'll have to ask Ben. It grew in the middle of our front lawn, and was the perfect climber. From the top branches, you could see the whole town. When Herbie was cut down, I thought about wearing a black armband as a mark of respect. What a tree!

Bombs at the pool: Executing a decent bomb from the one-metre board is another life skill that ALL KIDS WHO READ THIS BOOK NEED TO LEARN.

Remember, all bombs go better if your mouth is stuffed to overflowing with a toffee apple bar or killer python, bought from the canteen with your mum's money. This also sugars up the water for the enjoyment of other swimmers. My favourite bombs were:

The Coffin:
Lying back,
arms crossed
like Dracula

The Jackie/Horsey:
Legs and arms
extended, limbs
enter water first

The Can Opener:
One knee
held to chest

Nick-Knocking: In the olden days, we used to knock on our neighbours' front doors and then run away and hide. I am not suggesting you play this game. If you play it, and people find out you heard about it from me, the editor says I'll have to write out this book fifty times. [Editor: We're not kidding, Bob!] Please don't nick-knock. It's not fun or clever. [P.S. It is a little bit fun.] [P.P.S. But not very clever.]

These are the glorious, sunny memories of my childhood. Footy and cricket, frivolity and fun. I'm sure there were bad times, but not too many. Although I do remember the day I jumped into the front seat of Mum's old Kingswood. It was parked in the driveway. I was fooling around and accidentally knocked the handbrake off. The car started to roll. I panicked and tried to jump out of the car to push the Kingswood back up the drive. I was five. The car was older than that. And bigger. I got stuck half in the car and half out, as it accelerated down the drive.

I broke a piece of my scapula, which is up near your shoulder.

It's one of those important lessons from childhood: Don't jump out of moving cars.

3

In which the Murphys try
their luck with cats

I'm a dog person now. Not just a Dogs person, as in Western Bulldogs, although I'm definitely one of those! But I'm also a person who loves dogs. Our current family canine is Arthur. He's a sausage dog who can't swim and refuses to get his paws wet. Ever.

When I was little, the Murphys were a cat family. This story is a bit sad, and a bit funny, and a bit gross, so if you don't like sad, funny and gross, turn to the next chapter about school.

[Let's wait a moment while those people leave the page.]

Okay, fans of sad, funny and gross, it's just us now. This is what happened. We were visiting the cousins on Mum's side in Dandenong. I mentioned earlier that Mum is one of 14 kids, so I have A LOT OF COUSINS. How many cousins? Well, have you ever counted the grains of sand in a sandpit? No, neither have I. And I haven't counted my cousins either.

[P.S. Yes, I have: I have 23,530 cousins.]

[P.P.S. That's not true, I actually have 354 cousins.]

[P.P.P.S. Whoops, untrue again, the real number is 127.]

[P.P.P.P.S. That actually isn't true. I have 67. I'm sorry I lied before.]

[P.P.P.P.P.S. Why don't you believe me? Okay, I'll list them at the end of the chapter.]

We arrived back in Warragul quite late. Ben, Brig and I were asleep in the back of the car. Or maybe we were pretending to be asleep so that Mum or Dad would carry us into the house and tuck us into bed. (Being carried to bed is the best!) Anyway, after we were in bed, Mum made a gruesome discovery. Shaka, our beloved cat, had been hit by a car and killed!

Poor Shaka! Mum figured that we kids would be devastated if we saw her, so she issued a blunt order to Dad: 'Go bury the cat!'

The next morning, I woke up to a big commotion coming from the backyard. Mum and Brig were out there, and from the sound of things all was not well.

I stepped into the backyard.

I wiped the sleepy sand from my eyes.

My jaw flapped open in total disbelief.

There was a dead cat sticking out of the ground.

Dad can do a lot of things well. He is a terrific teacher. He is a first-class story-teller. He's a truly brilliant dad. But that day we learnt there was one thing he wasn't so great at – burying cats.

He'd gone out there, late at night, and dug a shallow grave that only fit the *front half* of Shaka (head, chest and arms). Meanwhile, the back half of Shaka was sticking out of the ground!

I'll say it again. Poor Shaka. He'd gone all stiff in the night as rigor mortis set in. So that was the scene. Brig shrieking. A cat's butt pointing to the heavens, his tail extended long and stiff like the handle of a golf club.

Mum decided that she would take charge. She stepped forward and seized Shaka by the tail. Her plan was to pull Shaka out and dig a proper grave for him.

She grabbed hold of Shaka's tail and pulled.

Nothing happened. Our half-buried cat stayed firmly in the ground.

She gripped harder and pulled again. Still Shaka didn't budge.

The third time, Mum really put her back into it. She grunted. She groaned, she leaned back like she was in tug of war, and . . . PULLED THE FUR RIGHT OFF SHAKA'S TAIL!

Mum stared at the fur sock in her hand. We stared at Mum. Then we looked at Shaka's exposed furless tailbone and backside, still sticking out of the dirt! Brig ooooohed. Mum shrieked. I stood there in stunned silence.

Poor, poor Shaka. He was eventually given a proper burial in the backyard. We said some nice words, and it was all very respectful and dignified.

RIP Shaka. And RIP Paddy too, who lasted longer than Shaka, but died when Dad accidentally ran over him in the driveway.

There's a saying that cats have nine lives. That wasn't really the Murphy experience.

But the other saying is: there's more than one way to skin a cat.

That one we can relate to.

MY COUSINS

Lucy, Anna, Maria, Dominic, Dave,
Nick, Joe, Ben, Steve, Brendan, Noel,
Gary, Narelle, Maureen, Frank, Peter,
Leonie, Bernice, Geoffrey, Anthony,
Martin, Leanne, Gerard, Sharyn,
Colleen, Gerald, Catherine, Bernard,
Margaret, James, Kieran, Leo, Paul,
Frank, Mark, Damian, Pauline, Nicholas,
Justin, Jacinta, Alison, Annette, Anne,
John, Karyn, David, Gillian, Simon,
Barrie, Robyn, Shane, Andrea, Michael,
Sue, Therese, Jane, Peter, Julie, Pam,
Deanne, Paul, Emma, David, John,
Tony, Lisa and Renae.

4

In which Bob talks like
an old man about grass

Grown-ups can be quite annoying talking about the olden days. I still remember what it sounded like as a kid: 'In our day, well, we didn't have no fancy computer whatsits. We had to make our own fun, with empty tin cans and dental floss!'

'When I was your age, there was no

playing till we'd done our chores. My job was to muck out the gully trap, with just me bare hands and a soup ladle! And I got sixpence!'

'Oh, what I wouldn't have given for this lovely tuna bake! In my day it was just sheep brains and spam on toast, and if you complained, Pa would put you over his knee!'

Well, let me turn into an old man for a moment and tell you about the St Joseph's Catholic Primary School oval.

Firstly, it wasn't an oval, it was a rectangle.

Secondly, we played no-holds-barred footy. Full contact, full tackling (no umpires, of course).

Thirdly, there was NOT A SINGLE BLADE OF GRASS, just gravel. Gravel that didn't just graze and scratch. Gravel that shredded. I remember looking down at my hands after a particularly nasty tackle and seeing little stones lodged deep in my palms!

Ah, the good old days. You kids don't learn important life skills anymore, like how to pick small rocks out of your bloodied hands.

The scariest tackler was Adam 'Blacky' Blackwood. Blacky was a year older than me, but at least a foot shorter. If I ever won the ball, Blacky would fly at me, like a dog waiting by the gate for the postman. Stocky and fierce, he tackled like a

Rottweiler. If he could sling a kid into the cyclone fence that circled the gravel, that was okay by Blacky. People often ask if I was scared playing AFL footy. Never as scared as I was playing on the gravel against Blacky.

We got better together. We were coached by our teacher, Mr Osler. I remember when we played in the primary school footy championships, he did the whole David and Goliath talk.

'Look at those fancy city kids with their fancy city footy grounds and all that *lush green grass*! What have we got?'

'Gravel!' we'd scream.

'I didn't hear ya! What have we got?'

'Gravel!'

'Well, go out there and show them how tough we are!'

Something must have worked. By the time I was in Grade 5 we were crowned the best primary school footy team in the state. I still remember a lot of my teammates. Leigh Baldry, our star player and son of a Shield cricketer. Ben 'Killer' Kilday, with his red hair and magnificent hands. Josh Vansittart, my best school friend and as brave as any footballer I ever played with.

Then there was Damian 'Gargs' Gargan. Gargs was light-framed and a bit timid. He might not have been the best player in the school, but he wore a special badge of honour.

Gargs' dad wasn't a rock star. Gargs' dad

wasn't prime minister. Gargs' dad wasn't
the first man to walk on the moon. It was
bigger than that.

Gargs' dad had played ACTUAL BIG-
TIME VFL footy. His name was in a book:

MICHAEL GARGAN,
NORTH MELBOURNE,
3 GAMES

I used to read that book and gawp.

League footy, imagine that.

5

In which Bob meets a girl
at the pool, and nothing is
ever the same

There were girls at high school. There'd been girls at primary school too, but I'd mainly left them alone to do handstands and talk about horses. At high school, girls stood out.

They had such nice faces, and they

smelled better than us. We boys sweated it up playing footy on the oval every lunchtime, which didn't help our smell cause. The girls would sit at the side of the oval, flicking their hair and organising their pencil cases. I played my heart out in case one of them glanced up from their Derwents and noticed me.

In truth, they were watching Simon Murnane, who was tanned and muscly and looked like the star of a shampoo commercial. I was scrawny and skinny and looked like a stick insect scampering away from a predator.

Now, hopefully the girls join in the footy game. With the explosion of women's footy, hopefully *everyone* stinks after sweaty lunchtimes playing footy on the oval.

Anyway, this chapter is about *a* girl. The most beautiful and wonderful girl I ever met.

I can hear some of you yelling across the pages of this book. 'Urrrrrrrgh! Lay off the mushy stuff, Bob! I'm only reading this book because I want to know what it's like playing with Marcus Bontempelli! Don't get all kissy kissy on us! Yuuuuuuuck!'

I understand your point of view, so I'll be quick.

I fell for Justine Quigley the moment I saw her. She had a small ponytail and a streak of red dye in her hair. She was also impossibly old. I was a Year 7. Justine was a Year 8.

For a while she barely noticed me.

Then, I sat next to Justine at the school swimming carnival. That was the day she worked out who I was. I was the kid who was so pale and skinny he was afraid to take his shirt off to swim a race. I was the kid desperately trying to impress her.

That day, conversation came easily. We talked about everything. We laughed a lot. Occasionally I got up to swim a race. Every time, I hurried back to sit on the grass next to the incredible Justine Quigley.

The swimming carnival was always a fun day. There was constant chanting and cheering. The energy somehow carried me along.

TOPICS FOR CONVERSATION
WITH JUSTINE

- How I was waaaayyyy better
  at athletics than swimming.

- How my mum was Year 7 coordinator
  so I knew all sorts of stuff.

- Whether Richmond should move
  Michael 'Butch' Gale to half back
  (dodgy topic, I moved on quickly).

By the end of the day, I was fully in love with Justine Quigley. To her, I was still a little Year 7, but I got the sense she liked me too. She told me a sad thing about herself. She said her dad had died in a car accident four years earlier. The words just thudded into me. It was the worst possible thing I could imagine. I saw that she wanted to cry, and I wanted to give her a hug.

We became friends that day. Not boyfriend and girlfriend, but close friends. We would pass notes to each other in the schoolyard. Even now, there is nothing on earth that has come close to the excitement of Justine pressing a letter into my palm as we crossed paths.

Okay, stop groaning! I've nearly finished.

We were friends right through high school.

By the time I got drafted, she was my best female friend.

She went away for a while.

She came back.

We got together.

We got married.

We had three kids – Jarvis, Frankie and Delilah.

Isn't that nice? Seriously, stop gagging. It's a beautiful love story.

And because you've been so patient, let me now tell you what it's like playing with Marcus Bontempelli.

WHAT IT'S LIKE PLAYING WITH MARCUS BONTEMPELLI

• The Bont is something close to the perfect footballer. He walks out of packs in slow motion, like he's walking in deep water.

• He competes rain, hail or shine.

• He uses his body and his brain to win the ball.

• He makes his teammates better by putting them into space with a handball or kick.

• He knows when the game needs a big moment and puts his mind to creating the moment!

6

In which Bob confesses a deep
love for the smell of leather

I like sniffing footies. This might sound weird, but if you like sniffing footies, you'll be saying, 'Of course Bob likes sniffing footies. It's obvious. Doesn't everyone love sniffing footies?' That's the thing. Once you become a footy sniffer, it's hard to imagine being anything else.

I don't just sniff any old footy. It's new footies that are particularly sniff-worthy. I like to cuddle a freshly minted Sherrin to my chest and take a deep breath.

MY TOP FIVE FOOTY SMELLS

1. A brand new footy

2. Liniment

3. Dubbin

4. Jam donuts

5. Vicks

I also like the smell of footies that have been polished with Dubbin. Dubbin is a special ointment for footies and boots. You rub its oily resin gently into the old leather and it becomes waxy and shiny and waterproof. The scuff marks disappear. It's the same as a makeover session that girls do with skincare products but for footies.

My dad was the Lord High Priest of Dubbin in the greater city of Warragul. The night before every game, he'd cradle my boots like a baby, attacking each dirty mark, working his Dubbiny magic. The next morning they'd be waiting for me, sparkling like new.

The mornings were almost always cold out in Gippsland. Through rain, wind and fog, Dad drove me to games. We'd play music in the car. Sometimes we'd talk. He had his three rules for footy: 'Hold your chest marks, kick with both feet, and man up!'

My first junior team was the Warragul Colts. Dad remembers me spending the first minutes of my first game watching from outside the pack. I'd been playing basketball for a while, and Dad wondered if I was too timid for footy. But then it clicked. The ball jarred loose and I swooped on it. I dodged through some traffic and hit a teammate with a pass. Dad thought, *He's got it, he's got the gift!*

I loved it so much. It wasn't just the games, the thrill of the contest, the challenge to improve. I loved hanging out with the kids in my team. I remember one Lightning Premiership where we spent every minute between games sliding down a mud bank.

Our coach was Frank Ahern. Frank was an old-school coach, who didn't complicate things too much for us Under 10s. His mantra was 'Kick it into the open spaces and be prepared to run'. I ran and kicked and practised and dreamt. The dream was always the same. One day I want to play AFL footy.

Dubbin, boots, Dad, Colts, Frank Ahern. This is the origin story of my footy life.

Give me a footy to smell, and I'm nine years old again, with all those dreams and possibilities.

Yes, I love sniffing footies.

7

In which Bob walks
on sacred ground

I guess I knew I was pretty good.

You never want to be boastful or get ahead of yourself but, like almost every footballer who goes on to play in the AFL, I knew fairly early on that I was a decent player. I could run fast and use both feet. I could read the game and knew where to go to get the ball. I won best and fairest trophies. I was selected for inter-league and combined school teams.

Some kids are mathsy, some kids are musical. Some kids are creative writers, some kids are comedians.

I was a footy kid.

I still remember the first time I had a big footy disappointment. When I became eligible to play for the Gippsland Power in the Under 18s, I wasn't invited to join the squad. Five other kids at my school were asked, but not me.

I remember thinking I was as good or better than those other kids.

I remember feeling the sting of injustice.

It lit a fire in me.

A month later I was given a late invite, and I trained harder than I ever had in my life. I made the Gippsland Power list, and the team, even though I was still a bottom-aged player (Under 17).

I later learnt that the coach of the Power, Peter Francis, deliberately made me wait. He knew that I was talented, but wondered whether my attitude was a little laidback. My late inclusion was designed to fire me up! It worked, and it's possible I have Peter Francis to thank for all that came afterwards.

I improved steadily over that first season in the Under 18s. I was given jobs on older and bigger opponents. Recruiters came to watch our games, with their clipboards and suspicious eyes. Gippsland started winning. In the end, we went all the way to the MCG on Grand Final Day!

What a day that was. The actual MCG. The theatre of my dreams. The actual grass. The actual seats. The air. The changing rooms. The scoreboard. Richo had walked here. Ablett too. Sir Donald Bradman had walked here! Every footballer and cricketer who was anybody had walked here. And now skinny Bob Murphy from Warragul was walking onto the sacred turf.

There was nobody there to watch. The Under 18s Grand Final started at 9 am, five and a half hours before the Kangaroos took on Carlton in the big one. But that didn't matter.

FIVE THINGS YOU NEED
TO KNOW ABOUT THE MCG

1. The grass is perfect.

2. In the twilight it feels like you're
   playing in a dream.

3. It's just as magical when it's empty.

4. The crowd noise lifts and swings like
   the swell of the deep blue ocean.

5. The ground feels small (probably
   because the grandstand is so big).

The MCG is just as glorious with nine
spectators as 90,000.

It didn't even matter that we lost. The
Sandringham Dragons beat us by more
than eight goals.

All that mattered was the dream.

The dream had lit up like the Olympic cauldron that once blazed over the MCG.

I was going to be an AFL footballer one day.

I really was.

Maybe.

Hopefully.

I really was maybe hopefully going to be an AFL footballer one day.

8

In which Bob (in his lucky
boxer shorts) goes
chasing Tigers

For most of my childhood, we were hopeless. The Tigers had won premierships just before I was born, but we were also-rans right through my primary school years.

We lost so many more than we won.

We never made the finals.

In 1989, it even looked like the Tigers might become extinct! Richmond had to rattle tins to raise money to stay in the competition. 'Save Our Skins', it was called. My future team, the Western Bulldogs, almost merged around the same time. It was a scary period to be short on money at the wrong end of the ladder.

It's sweet, though, when it turns around.

For the Tigers, that happened in 1995. The reason, we all reckoned, was Richo.

Richo doesn't need another name. Richo was an athlete, a demigod, a superhero, an aerialist, an entertainer, a personality, a star. He ran with high knees and flowing hair. At his best he was completely unstoppable. At his worst, he would get stroppy with everyone and kick points. But he's kicked more goals on the MCG than any other player. At the very end of his career, when everyone thought he might be finished, he shifted to the wing and almost won the Brownlow.

Richo is now on the telly, helping with special comments on Saturday nights. Every time I see him, there's a little part of my heart that still leaps. *That's Richo,* I think. I can't believe *I* get to talk to *Richo*, that he's my *friend*!

Imagine if I could tell ten-year-old Robbie that *we become friends* with Richo. He'd wet his yellow-and-black boxer shorts!

In 1995, the Murphys started travelling to the MCG to watch the Tigers. We had our routine. I'd wear my Tigers jumper and scarf. We'd park in the backstreets of Richmond before the game. Then we'd begin the walk to the 'G'. Dad was always 10 or 20 or 30 metres in front. The rest of us were almost jogging as we tried to keep up. The Tiger army swept us along. There was a vibe of anticipation and nervous energy. The Murphys were in the big city! With Dad as our leader, we were drawn towards the great lights of the MCG like insects.

'Slow down!' Mum would yell at Dad. He'd try to slow down but would quickly speed up again.

Eventually, the game would start. We'd sit behind the goals at the Ponsford Stand end. That 1995 season, the Tigers were so exciting. We won the first nine games. Richo did his knee at the SCG in Round 10. We finished the home-and-away season in third place. I wore Wayne Campbell's number 9, but I loved them all.

FIVE THINGS MY DAD YELLS AT THE FOOTY

1. 'They don't want it!' — response to fierce tackling and opposition coughing up the ball.

2. 'Wrighty!' — as in, former Magpie wingman Graeme Wright.

3. 'Ball?!'

4. 'Yeah!'

5. 'Look at him go!'

We won our first final against Essendon, after being five goals down. Matthew Knights kicked three in the first half. That was one of my favourite days ever. On the drive home to Warragul, we smiled the whole way, my Tigers scarf flapping out the window triumphantly.

The next week, Richmond lost the preliminary final to Geelong by 15 goals.

But I didn't care.

The Tigers had arrived!

We were surely going to win the flag in 1996!

And in a few years, I'd be winning flags with Richmond too. Because surely the Tigers would realise that I was a true believer, right down to the Matthew Knights badge on my duffel coat?

Of course, that part of the dream didn't happen.

I wasn't destined for the Tigers.

And maybe that's not a bad thing.

After the joy of '95, Richmond only played in one finals series in 17 years!

Ouch.

9

In which a boy becomes a Dog

In June of 1999, I received a letter.

I know what some of you kids are thinking. 'Tell us more, Bob. What's this "letter" thing of which you speak?'

Well, it goes like this. In the olden days, before email and Snapchat, people used to write actual physical *letters* to each other. You'd stick a stamp on them and the postie delivered them to the letterbox out the front of your house. It was magic! Slow, old-fashioned magic.

So, in 1999 I received a letter. It wasn't just any letter. It was a letter from the Brisbane Lions Football Club. I do not remember the exact words, but it encouraged me to nominate for the upcoming national draft.

I jumped for joy on the sofa!

I whooped like I was five years old!

I flapped the letter at Mum like I was Charlie Bucket waving a golden ticket.

Somebody had noticed me playing for the Gippsland Power. I might actually be a chance to be drafted, come November!

After the Brisbane Lions approach, other

clubs contacted me too. On the morning of the draft, there was an article in the paper predicting the Top 10. There I was at number 10! 'Robert Murphy, skinny as skinny'. My actual name in the actual paper! 'Skinny as skinny' wasn't overly flattering, but who cared!

I was *this close* to my AFL dream.

After all the fuss, surely my name would be called out?

Surely I'd end the day tied to an AFL club?

One of the main possibilities was West Coast. The Eagles had picks 11 and 14 and had said they were keen. Mum and Dad were a bit nervous that I might be moving away to the other side of the country.

I was less concerned. But I preferred to stay in Victoria.

The Western Bulldogs was one of the best possibilities. Scott Clayton, the Bulldogs recruiter, had spoken to me at Draft Camp. He'd whisked me away behind the basketball courts and had a quick, secretive chat.

'Are you keen to come to the Doggies?' he whispered, like we were in a spy film.

'Yes, I am,' I whispered back.

'How tall are your parents, son?'

I could tell Scott was sizing up my narrow frame. Would I get any bigger? Would I have the physique to survive AFL football?

'Dad is 187 cm and Mum is 179.'

I spotted them an extra five centimetres

each. Look, a kid's gotta do what a kid's gotta do.

It must have worked. The Eagles took future captain Darren Glass at pick 11. Then Port took Paul Koulouriotis at 12. At my family home, 186 Albert Road, Warragul, two dozen people sat forward in nervous silence.

'Pick 13, Western Bulldogs ... Robert Murphy, Gippsland Power.'

Pandemonium. The crowd of relatives, neighbours and family friends in my living room erupted. I was squeezed into many a weeping, congratulatory hug. The phone went into meltdown. In those first few minutes, I received a call from Bulldogs coach Terry Wallace.

'Congratulations,' he said. 'The hard work starts now.'

The Murphys hosted a decent party that night. Justine came over. She wasn't my girlfriend yet, but she was the girl of my dreams. Do you want me to go on about it like I did in the other chapter?

'Nooooooo!'

Are you sure?

'Yeeeeeees!'

Okay, I'll tell you about Connie Matthews instead then. Connie was our neighbour. She was an elderly woman, and her husband Bob had played reserves footy for the Dogs back in the day. He'd been a barber for many years, just down the road from Whitten Oval. Bob had died not long before the draft, and when Connie hugged me her eyes were full of tears. I would meet so many wonderful Dogs fans in my years as a player. Connie was the first.

I celebrated getting drafted like it was the greatest thing that had ever happened to me. Because it was! For a 17-year-old, how exciting can you get? One day you're collecting footy cards. The next day you're *on* a footy card.

If it ever happens to you, promise me one thing.

Don't be cool. Don't be professional. Don't spout clichés.

Go berserk!

Smile your biggest smile, hug the people you love, and punch the air.

The draft is the drawbridge to the dream. Hardly anybody gets to walk across. On the 1st of November 1999, I was one of the lucky ones.

10

In which Bob leaves home
to live in a kennel

Those first few months as a Western Bulldogs draftee were both exhausting and exhilarating.

Let's start with exhilarating. Think of all the cool things that might happen if you become an AFL footballer. A lot of those things *really do* happen.

Here's a list of five totally cool things that happened to me.

FIVE TOTALLY COOL THINGS THAT HAPPENED TO ME

1. Gear — It's all free! Within minutes of arriving at the club, I had tracksuits, training tops, sports bags, runners. Most exciting of all was jumper presentation night, when I was given my first official number.

2. Stars — Champion footballers from the TV are all around you! Every day! In 1999, the Dogs' biggest stars were probably Chris Grant and Nathan Brown. But there was also Tony Liberatore and Scott Wynd, who'd both won Brownlow Medals. There was Brad Johnson, a jet on the rise. And the guy who drove me to

training each day was Luke Darcy. Darc was an absolute gun. Suddenly I'm just in his car, listening to Red Hot Chili Peppers CDs, chatting like we're old mates. It was unreal.

3. Footy card photos — I know I've made a big deal of this, BUT YOU REALLY DO GET TO BE ON A FOOTY CARD!

4. Signing autographs — When you first arrive, you're not a familiar face so you're not swamped for autographs. Those first few times, it's an absolute thrill. Sometimes I wondered if the supporter was just being polite. 'I don't know who you are but you're standing next to Brad Johnson so I'll ask you too.'

5. Salary — I definitely wasn't in it for the money, and new recruits didn't get paid like the older guys. But we still got $500 a week. I was in Year 12.

5. (cont.) My friends at Marist Sion
who were working at **KFC** got
$12 an hour!

But apart from all that cool stuff, it was hard too.

The training was exhausting. Those early months were some of the most stressful of my life. I'd moved out of home. Warragul was just too far from Footscray. But I figured that if you're on a footy card, you maybe shouldn't be living with your mum.

A rookie's body is never ready for that first preseason. There are lots of difficult things you face in that first year too. Here are five of them.

FIVE DIFFICULT THINGS ABOUT YOUR FIRST YEAR IN AFL

1. Pain — Preseason is about pushing your body to get it ready for extraordinary demands. Some of the activities hurt a lot! Whether it's running 10 x 1km time trials, or doing maximum chin-ups, you have to push through pain. It's hard! The easier thing to do is quit. Some mornings, you arrive at the club and think, 'Do I have to run until I feel like vomiting today?'

2. Fear — My main fear was failing in front of my teammates. My endurance was often at its limit, and I was scared that my teammates would see my body fail. In actual fact, older players know what it's like for younger players, and they normally want to help. But it's a competitive environment. Nobody wants to be a quitter.

3. Shyness — I wasn't shy, but I did feel like a newbie. When you're a new face, and you've never played a game, you can tell everyone is assessing you. You don't quite fit in yet. You're not completely part of the team.

4. Feeling judged — You go from hanging out with kids, to adults who are judging your every effort. It's a new peer group, a new pressure, and it takes a while to get used to.

5. Time — It feels like you have no time to yourself. No time for friends, girlfriends, socialising, going out, seeing family. All you do is eat, sleep, train. Eat, sleep, train. Repeat. Forever.

In my first year, I was also doing Year 12 at Footscray City College. I did the bare minimum number of subjects and fit everything around footy. But it was a very full program. Sometimes I'd sit in the spa after a training session, and just *fall asleep* – right there in the hot tub!

This was a typical Wednesday:

6–7.30 am – Weights at the club.

9–3.30 am – Full day of school classes, no free periods.

4.15 pm – Picked up by teammate Simon Atkins for training at Werribee (Bulldogs VFL team).

9.30 pm – Home.

Our coach at Werribee was Alastair Clarkson. Most people would now say that

Clarkson is the greatest AFL coach of the modern era, so it wasn't a bad place to start!

I improved week after week.

I was named as emergency for the senior team eight weeks in a row.

My mind and body rose to the challenge of playing against adult men, not just boys.

Then, after training on a crisp winter night in July 2000, coach Terry Wallace called the whole group in to say, 'I want to congratulate Murph, he's going to be making his debut on Saturday.'

All the players shook my hand, and some of them hugged me.

I sat in front of my locker for a long time after everyone had left. Thinking about the game. Thinking about what I'd say to Mum and Dad. Knowing that life would never be the same after Saturday.

11

In which Robert Murphy of
Warragul, Victoria, becomes
an AFL footballer

The 15th of July 2000. That was a day I'll never forget.

I woke up early. I ate my Weetbix and banana and honey. I went to the shop and bought the paper. I pretended to read an article or two. Who was I kidding.

I flicked straight to the footy teams section at the back.

And there it was, in black and white:

IN R. Murphy (New, Gippsland Power).

We were playing Carlton at Princes Park. The Blues were a powerful team. They'd won 13 in a row and sat second on the ladder. The previous year, they'd played in the Grand Final.

I arrived at the ground two hours before the game. Everyone in the rooms shook my hand and said good luck. In the pre-match, we did all that gee-up stuff. Push-ups, high knee jumps, counting to ten loudly. I was nervous that I might not keep it together. Maybe I'd get out there and be unable to kick the ball in the line drill.

COOL THINGS THAT HAPPEN
IN THE CHANGE ROOMS WHEN
YOU'RE IN THE TEAM

• Boots are cleaned and polished by the
property steward. Dad didn't have to
do it anymore!

• Great massages — trainers have magic
hands.

• You feel special — when the coach
calls the meeting, you're in there.
You're in the inner sanctum.

• You get given a copy of *The Footy
Record* to read.

• It's exciting. It feels like everyone's
watching. It's on **TV**, a crowd is
building. It's a thrill!

The crowd that day was 25,397. When we ran onto the ground and through the banner, my body surged with adrenaline. If you'd given me a cape and some tights, I might have taken flight! I was almost afraid to look around in case all those fans spooked me. I looked at the grass, the sky. I clung to the warm-up footy I was holding for dear life.

Finally, the game got underway.

It was like stepping into the television screen at Mum and Dad's. All those heroes. All those big names.

And it wasn't just big names. It was big dudes. I tried not to look at their massive thighs and ripped torsos. I still had the physique of a weedy teenager. Even later

in my career, muscles weren't really my thing. But in that first game, I was a pipe cleaner in boots!

At one point a fight broke out. The big men grunted and wrestled and swore and scragged. Maybe out of respect for the spindly first-gamer, they left me alone. That suited me! The fight moved around me like I was a rock in a stream.

It ended up being a famous game in the history of the Western Bulldogs.

In the dying minutes, Scott West shovelled a handball out to me and I was all on my own. I drifted in close and wobbled a mongrel punt straight through. I'd kicked the goal to put us in front! A few minutes later, the siren sounded. We'd won by three points! We'd beaten a powerhouse of the competition, on their own deck!

'Sons of the West, red, white and blue!' The song blared out across this field of dreams.

Simon Garlick, one of the team leaders, put me in a headlock and growled, 'Where have you been all year?'

That's the moment I felt I belonged.

12

In which Bob learns not to sit
at the front in team meetings
after disappointing losses

When the coach yells at you, it's called 'a spray'.

I think it's because the insults fire out of their mouths like a spray of bullets. Maybe it's because they lose control of their saliva and start spitting everywhere.

THREE SIGNS YOU'RE RECEIVING A SPRAY

1. Coach is pointing at you and yelling.

2. Veins are bulging out on coach's forehead.

3. Coach is calling you by your first name, like you're in trouble with a parent.

Every AFL footballer has been on the receiving end of a spray. I strongly believe that young footballers shouldn't receive sprays. Encouragement works much better than abuse when you're first starting out. It's even possible that encouragement works better than abuse the whole way through your career!

But sprays make angry coaches feel

better. Sometimes they have to let it out.

I remember the day my first AFL coach, Terry Wallace, gave me an epic spray.

After the glory of the win against Carlton in my first game, we lost badly at Princes Park in 2001. I still hadn't played ten games. A lot of us performed poorly. It was a dirty day.

We sensed trouble the moment we walked off the field. 'Straight into the meeting room!' Plough yelled. We called Terry Wallace 'Plough'. Everyone did.

At the front of the room was a whiteboard. In one column were the names of players the coach thought had battled hard. In the other column, a list of the players who had not made enough of an effort.

It's amazing how quickly I found my own name.

Oh no, I was on the wrong side of the board!

Sure enough, when Terry Wallace got to me, he lost the plot. He talked about footy as if it was war. He said that I was a soldier who had not been 'up for the battle'.

'Murph, you were disgraceful! This war was fought toe-to-toe. Hand-to-hand combat! The enemy grabbed your knife out of your hands and stabbed you with it! BANG! YOU'RE DEAD!'

I was sitting right under the coach's nose. As the abuse poured out of him, he started to act out stabbing me with an imaginary blade!

One of the assistant coaches giggled.

Nobody dared look at me or Terry Wallace.

I was being pretend murdered in front of my teammates!

Eventually it finished, and I trudged off to lick my imaginary wounds.

I vowed to do better.

I didn't want to be on the wrong side of the whiteboard again.

I wanted to change what the coach thought of me.

13

In which Bob returns to
the land of his ancestors,
to be sure, to be sure

If you're wondering whether you have Irish heritage, take my quick 'Am I Irish?' spot quiz.

AM I IRISH?

- Is your favourite colour green?

- Does one of your parents have ten or more brothers and sisters?

- Does your surname begin with O'Something?

- Is your name Liam, Niamh, Siobhan, Sean, Shaun, Shawn or Shon?

- Does your mum or dad call a violin a 'fiddle'?

- Do you think a 'Hail Mary' is something other than a hopeful shot at goal in the dying seconds?

- Does your mum or dad worship Zach Tuohy, even though they don't like Geelong?

- Can your mum or dad spell 'Zach Tuohy' without looking it up?

- Do your parents barrack for Ned Kelly against the policemen?

- Do you go through a lot of sunscreen?

If you answered yes to five or more of these, you've probably got Irish blood.

I'm Australian – no doubt about it, mate! – but there's also no doubting my Irish blood. Mum is a Slattery, and all Slatterys trace their ancestors back to Ireland.

Dad is a Murphy, and the only name more Irish than Slattery is Murphy.

Mum has 13 brothers and sisters.

Dad loves to sing 'Danny Boy'.

Yes, I'm Australian, but my heritage is as Irish as a big, brown, knobbly potato.

So it was extremely exciting when I was picked to tour Ireland with the Australian international rules team. It was 2002 and I was still only in my third year as a player. I remember the thrill of training and playing with the competition's elite.

Shane Crawford was captain, and Chris Judd, Nathan Brown, Matthew Scarlett and Adam Simpson were in the team. One of our teammates was the sublimely talented West Coast star Daniel Kerr. He had some skill with the round ball too. Seventeen years later, his little sister, Samantha Kerr, is arguably the best round-ball footballer in the world.

I remember travelling to a rough part of Dublin for our warm-up game against Dublin City. As our bus rolled into the car park behind the pitch, I heard a *Whack! Whack! Whack!*

Something was hitting the bus windows!

I peered out and saw a bunch of kids standing a few metres away with arms cocked. They were pinging stones at our bus! Those cheeky little rascals were our unofficial welcome party.

I looked closer at these pint-sized hooligans. They were about six to ten years old. They had mousey brown hair. They had red cheeks and freckle-dotted faces. They looked familiar. They looked like me, ten years earlier! *Oh boy, I really am Irish*, I thought.

Pretty soon, the Irish players and spectators were letting me know the same thing. When my Dublin City opponent saw the name printed on my shirt he said, 'Murphy! You should be playin' for us, ya turncoat!'

When I sat on the bench, the crowd

behind us started getting involved. 'Murphy, ya bleedin' traitor! You're a tray-tor!'

It was all said tongue-in-cheek. The Irish were having a laugh. My teammates were laughing too. It was the beginning of the trip of a lifetime.

We won the first test at Croke Park in front of nearly 50,000 Irish fans. In the second test, my Bulldogs buddy Luke Darcy scored the team's only netted goal (6-pointer). And I scored an 'over' (a lofted goal over the net, worth 3 points). The test ended in a tie, 42 points each!

I'll never forget the sound of 71,544 frenzied Irish fans going bananas. We won the test series, and Ireland won this boy's heart.

I went home with a love of Irish music, Irish humour, Irish pubs and Irish people.

I vowed to get back there, and to show the country to Justine.

It was like finding a second home, halfway across the world.

14

In which Bob doesn't go
on a fishing trip

We knew the 2004 preseason was going to be tough. In 2003, we were wooden-spooners. We'd only won three games. When you've had a poor season, the coach normally wants to make you pay with sweat and lactic acid.

I remember when the note went out for

the preseason camp. The location was a secret, but we were told to bring golf clubs.

And a fishing rod.

Some of the boys were hopeful. 'This might not be too bad. Maybe some hard running in the morning, then nine holes in the afternoon.'

We arrived at dawn on the Monday morning of camp. We sat in the meeting room. Nobody said a word. It was tense. We had an inkling something was up.

Then, at precisely 6 am, three army guys burst into the room! They were wearing the full special ops gear. They just stood braced at the front of the room and stared at us. They had ice in their eyes and guns on their hips!

I bit my lip. We clearly weren't going on a fishing trip.

A few minutes later we were face-down on Whitten Oval, doing push-ups. The special ops guys were yelling at us. They didn't call me 'Bob'. They didn't call me 'Bobby' or 'Rob' or 'Robbie' or 'Murph' either. They called me 'Blue 5'. That's who I was, for the rest of the camp.

Team Blue, Number 5.

At some point, Blue 5 could not do any more push-ups. The special ops guys didn't like this. They yelled at Blue 5 to toughen the hell up!

We did more push-ups in front of the bus. This time I ate asphalt when I couldn't endure any more pain.

Then we were on the bus. Nobody spoke. We just glanced at each other nervously.

The first stop was Port Melbourne beach. What followed were the most physically challenging 120 minutes of my life.

Blue 5 was made to jump into the sea in his clothes.

Blue 5 had to heave a rope through chest-deep waves.

Blue 5 carried logs over the sand.

Blue 5 did dips on the handrails, burpees in the sand, and push-ups until his puny arms collapsed.

And Blue 5 did sit-ups. So many that eventually his abdomen seized up in cramps.

'You call those sit-ups?!' the special ops guy roared.

I was in too much pain to speak. I was cooked.

'I can't actually move,' I croaked as the special ops guy walked away.

At that point, Blue 4, whose real name was Simon Garlick, got the giggles. In the distant future, Simon would become the CEO – the big boss – of the Western Bulldogs, but that day he was just Blue 4. He saved me with his laughter. He whispered a few jokey military commands, all of which ended with 'Sir!'

It was dangerous stuff, but just what I needed.

The blue team ended up linking arms to help me finish my sit-ups. Garlo became my friend for life.

The rest of the camp was at a place called Mount Disappointment. It really was! You don't believe me, do you? I went through hell at Mount Disappointment. It was disappointing, to say the least.

I'll never forget those two and a half days. We were broken and rebuilt. We learnt about resilience. We relied on each other to get through it all. The camp ended with abseiling down cliff-faces, and team-building exercises.

That camp was something close to torture.

I honestly wouldn't have got through it without Blue 4.

We learnt something about belonging to a team and supporting each other.

And then we got on the bus, exhausted, and went back to the club to collect our fishing rods.

THE FIVE PHYSICALLY HARDEST THINGS TO DO ON A FOOTY FIELD

1. Sit-ups (for me, anyway).

2. Chasing a fast wingman.

3. Tackling a superstar like Patrick Dangerfield.

4. Taking a high mark over a ruckman like Aaron Sandilands.

5. Trying to run fast after you've been wrestling a tagger.

15

In which Bob hears the
sickening sound of Velcro

It was already a dirty night. We were trailing the Pies on a Friday at the MCG. Destined to lose by 34 points.

In the blur of play, the ball was shunted along in my direction. I took possession. I saw Collingwood man-mountain Anthony Rocca charging.

The mantra 'Keep your feet' had always served me well. I dug my feet into the ground. My legs went rigid.

The man-mountain collected me. Twisted me. Threw me to the ground.

My feet stayed where they'd been planted. Not forever – that would be truly gruesome – but for far, far too long.

My left knee was ripped apart.

You know the sound of Velcro ripping? That is what I heard as my ACL – one of the most important bands of tissue holding the knee together – tore.

You know the feeling of ripping a drumstick from the body of a roast chook? It was that wrenching sensation that came with the horrible sound.

Pain flooded into my knee. A deep ache throbbed into the joint. Then it disappeared. No sound. No pain. Nothing.

I knew my knee was cactus. The club doctor arrived on the field and performed 'the test'. The test is a short, sharp jolt of the knee by the doctor's hands to see if the ACL is still there to catch the knee.

I could see in his eyes that mine wasn't.

I was eased onto a stretcher and then rolled across the field of play. I stared at the black sky and tried to keep the heaving panic at bay.

I'd done my knee.

All the work, all the preparation. All the hopes for the season, for the next 12 months.

I'd done my knee.

I felt the sting of tears, like I was still a little kid. But you don't really want to bust out the tears on national TV. I concentrated on the black sky.

The crowd clapped as the stretcher neared the boundary. When you hear that quiet, respectful clapping, you know for sure that your knee is cactus.

When we reached the gate, I looked around for Justine. We'd recently become a couple. The girl from the swimming carnival was finally my girlfriend.

I scanned the crowd. No Justine. All I saw as I left the field were concerned Bulldogs faces.

Even the Collingwood faithful were

subdued. Nobody wants to see a serious injury.

Then I saw a freckly-faced young kid lean over the fence. He was wearing his black-and-white jumper and was about nine years old.

'Hey, Murphy,' he said, clearly loud enough for me to hear. 'Murphy – you really stuffed my Dreamteam!'

Man, that's harsh, I thought. My knee lies in tatters and this kid wants to complain about fantasy football!

I should have sat up on the stretcher and said, 'This is on you, young fella. You should have saved your trades!'

But I didn't say anything.

I was just wheeled silently into the

tunnel, to start 12 months out of the game
I loved so much.

16

In which Bob sees the future
in wonky black capitals

In the early days of my career, I'm not sure many people thought of me as captaincy material.

The great leaders of our club had the knack of fitting in. Like a school captain or a prefect, they did the right thing most of the time. They wore the club uniform smartly. They said the right things in meetings and press conferences. They set an example. They were proper grown-ups. Some of them, like my first captain, Scott Wynd, even seemed superhuman!

I liked to think I was a little rock 'n' roll. Not a rebel, because there isn't much room for rebels in professional footy, but a happy-go-lucky kid who ran to his own beat.

For example, there was a time early in my career when I didn't have a training bag to carry my gear in. I'd just rock up at the club with my boots and shorts, singlet and towel under my arm.

Eventually, my friend and mentor Luke Darcy suggested I should 'tidy up my professionalism'.

Slowly, I realised that being a leader doesn't mean being perfect. I learnt that it was okay to show the group that you weren't perfect. It's called 'vulnerability'.

I also learnt that leadership can work in many different shapes and sizes. Some captains are motivators, and masters of the three-quarter-time speech. Some are quieter, but make sure they know exactly what is going on in every teammate's life. Some are courageous and set the perfect example on the field for others to follow. Some are charismatic and people just love being around them. The greatest captains are all these things.

And they are selfless too. Great captains always put the team first.

It's hard for young players to be selfless. When you first make AFL footy, you are desperate just to keep getting a game. To cement YOUR spot. To fulfil YOUR dream.

As you get more established, it's easier to think about the greater good. And it's easier to think about the TEAM.

My interest in being a leader took a long time to mature. When it finally did, I became obsessed with leadership. What makes groups try harder? How can we achieve this premiership goal together? What are the best ways to communicate? How can we be more honest with one another?

The most important thing I realised was that it was okay to be me! I didn't have to be perfect. I didn't have to be Scott Wynd. I could be a leader within the team and still be myself.

Although I did have to get a training bag. The game was up on that front.

One of the great days in my football life was when I became captain of the Western Bulldogs. It was the 15th of October 2014. The club's president, Peter Gordon, invited me to his place to go for a walk with him. And on the walk, he told me he wanted me to be captain.

Here's a strange thing. Just after Peter offered me the job, we stopped on a footbridge. The Yarra River flowed beneath us. There was graffiti painted on the concrete of the bridge. And there, in wonky

CAPTAIN

black capitals, was spray-painted the word 'CAPTAIN'.

It was weird. Peter and I just stood and stared at it. The whole moment summed up by a bit of bridge graffiti.

I'd been a player for 15 seasons and 250 games. Yep, some kids take a bit longer to mature!

17

In which Bob talks about sticky tape and songs

One thing I love about footy are the run-through banners. Not many other sports have banners. They might have streamers. They might have dancers. They might even have fireworks.

But they don't have mountains of crepe paper in club colours held together by sticky tape, with giant portraits of footballers' heads.

They don't have diehard fans who do the art and craft during the week, then enter the arena to hold up their masterpiece against the wind and rain.

They don't have occasional misspellings.

They don't have messages like 'Lachie Hunter. 150 Scintillating Games'.

Yes, I love banners. They are a unique and fun tradition in Aussie rules.

When I first started playing AFL footy, I tried not to touch the banner. I'd run out behind somebody wider than me, which was pretty much everyone, and then duck through as the hole opened up. It was a superstition. I figured that it was bad luck to make contact with the banner itself.

Later on, I laughed when my cheeky teammate Nathan Brown would try to kick the ball through the milestone player's large cartoon head. Browny had a naughty streak. He was also one of the most brilliantly skilful footballers I ever saw. If Browny wanted to kick a footy through your massive crepe paper noggin, he could do it.

When I became captain, my superstitions went away. In fact, it was my greatest thrill in footy to lead the players out and through the banner first.

It wasn't always easy, though! Some days you'd sprint forward and just hit a wall of sticky tape!

Ouch.

I also love AFL club songs. Well, most of them, anyway (I'm looking at you, Freo (way to go)! And you, West Coast Eagles!)

If you ask AFL players what the best part of footy is, most will say, 'Singing the song after a win'.

How good are the original club anthems?

I love how they get a bit trumpety and brass bandy.

I love how they sound like they belong on great-grandad's gramophone.

I love how they have old-worldy lyrics like 'cakewalk' and 'Bulldog breed'.

The Western Bulldogs' song is 'Sons of the West'. It comes from an old sea shanty, 'Sons of the Sea'. Our rule is to never let a camera or any media inside our winning circle because it is a sacred place.

When players start out, they sometimes don't know the words.

You can get away with this for the debut win because you have a date with a Gatorade shower.

I liked watching other people get drenched in Gatorade, but hated getting it on myself. So sticky!

There is a different quality to the singing when it's a really important win, or one nobody expected. The players roar the song out.

It's absolutely spine-tingling.

I'll never forget one rendition after a game versus Sydney at the SCG in 2015. It was wet, and we trailed at three-quarter time. The last quarter was a soggy mud wrestle. The Swans kicked the first couple, but we somehow stayed in the game. Heading in to time on, Easton Wood jumped high to karate kick the ball towards the goal-line. The Swans defender lunged. Had it crossed the line?

Score review. Goal! We were in front by four points!

Somehow we hung on that day. The Swans had a late chance for a goal in the dying seconds but Easton Wood and Jason Johannisen and an exhausted Matty Boyd saved the day.

In the euphoria of that win, I had a feeling that great things were happening.

We had found our belief. We won when

everyone expected us to fold.

We sang the song that day as though we'd never get to sing it again. The victory circle was like a mosh pit at a rock festival. We linked arms and held onto each other and lurched violently from side to side.

Some of the singing wasn't up to the standard of the Australian Boys Choir – there is possibly no worse singer on this planet than Matthew Boyd – but that didn't matter.

But you can't beat the boys

of the Bulldog breed

We're the team of the mighty West!

Even now, it makes the hair stand up on the back of my neck.

18

In which Bob remembers the
three coaches who made him

My first AFL coach once dressed up as
Darth Vader for the pre-match meeting.

Terry Wallace is a footy nut. He was a
magnificent player for the Hawks, the
Bulldogs and the Tigers. I think he started
favourite in a couple of Brownlows.

As a coach, he was full of daring ideas.

He almost took the Doggies to the Grand Final in 1997, and again in 1998. That was just before my time.

The Darth Vader costume was just before my time too. The assistant coaches came as stormtroopers. The theme of that game was 'The Empire Strikes Back'. My former captain Brad Johnson still smiles when he talks about it. Mind you, Brad Johnson smiles at everything.

Sometimes, a coach has to be inventive to keep everyone listening.

Plough's most famous theme game in my time was the 'Mission Impossible' game in 2000. We were playing the Brisbane Lions, who were on their way to three premierships in a row.

On the Monday, Plough played the *Mission Impossible* theme song. He gave each of us a 'special assignment'. We were going to do what nobody thought we could do. We were all Tom Cruise.

We lost by seven goals. The mission really was impossible. Or at least very difficult. Which isn't to say I didn't appreciate Plough's theme. Coaches can only do so much.

Rodney 'Rocket' Eade was my coach for the most years at the Dogs. I loved playing under Rocket. He was a sharp tactician and a great storyteller. Between 2008 and 2010 he coached us to three preliminary finals for three losses.

He also loved a joke. A player once asked,

'Can you bring your dog to the team barbecue?' Quick as a flash, Rocket quipped, 'You don't want to bring your own dog?' We all laughed.

I finished under Luke Beveridge, who's still the coach of the Dogs. He'll forever be a club legend for coaching us to the 2016 premiership.

Bevo is a man like no other. He's a surfer, and a skateboarder. He's tough as nails, but he also loves a hug. He's deadly serious about footy, but he's also a joker.

I remember the day Bevo opened the pre-match before a big game with a gag:

'Fellas,' he said in a bad pirate accent. 'What is a pirate's favourite letter?'

A handful of his bewildered players

guessed, 'Rrrrrrrrr?'

'No,' said Bevo, still acting a very poor pirate. 'You think it's the Rrrrrrrr, but it's actually the Cccccccc.'

Get it? Favourite letter … C … Sea … Don't blame me! Although I admit I did laugh.

That's what he wanted. He wanted us to laugh. To relax for a moment. Footy is so often a serious business. Sometimes players need a bit of silliness.

Bevo was a master of that stuff. When to be serious. When to have a laugh. I thought of him as 'the coach I always wanted to have' and in 2015 I called him that in public. I'd found a kindred spirit for my footy soul.

Then came Grand Final Day 2016. But

that's a story for another chapter.

Bevo and I have a connection that will never be broken.

19

In which Bob dares to be
different — or at least
to be himself

One of the glorious things about being human is that none of us are exactly the same. I'm me. You're you. Nat Fyfe is Nat Fyfe. The fact that Nat is better at footy than you or me is just *one thing* about being Nat Fyfe! There are lots of others. He also swims in the ocean every morning, no matter how cold, and sometimes drives grain trucks around Western Australia!

Football clubs like to control players. If every player started telling the media exactly what he thought about everything, the club might implode with all that opinion! It would be mayhem.

Clubs pay footballers a lot of money, so they can set the rules. Clubs tell players what they can say, what they can't say, what they can eat, what they can't eat, and what time they have to wade through freezing water in their Speedos.

Unfortunately, all this control means that players start sounding like zombie aliens from Planet Cliché.

MY TOP FIVE MODERN FOOTY CLICHÉS

1. 'We stuck to our process.'

2. 'We all played our role.'

3. 'We got our structures right.'

4. 'We're just taking it one week at a time.'

5. 'We want to be a team that's hard to beat.' – DUH!

But it is possible to obey team rules and not be boring. Why not try to share a little of your personality when you get the chance?

Most past players who make it in the media are picked because they shared a little personality, despite all the dreaded 'media training'.

Whenever I had a chance to express myself as a player, I tried to use it well. To be myself!

The Player Profile

I adored filling out the Player Profile in *The Footy Record*. Here was a place I really could be myself.

Many footballers play it safe when it comes to the Player Profile. They say their favourite food is pasta and their favourite movie is *The Shawshank Redemption*. You might not have seen it yet. It's a great movie. The weird thing is that *so many* footballers say *Shawshank* is their favourite movie. What they're really saying is that they don't want to stand out.

My favourite movie is *Field of Dreams*. It's a beautiful sports movie about a corn farmer who builds a baseball diamond in the hope his favourite player will come and play. 'If you build it, he will come.' Man, I love that movie. I might go and watch it again now …

I also put down that my favourite food is phở. It's a fragrant Vietnamese breakfast soup. You pronounce phở as 'fuh'. There are a lot of Vietnamese restaurants around Footscray and Whitten Oval. I was happy to get that exotic-looking Vietnamese letter in phở in *The Footy Record*.

Under 'Dream Dinner Guests', I usually chose Australian comedians and musicians, just in case they read the profile and asked me out to dinner. This actually happened once! I rocked up at a café called Tiamo in Lygon Street and two of my favourite local musicians, Tim Rogers and Tex Perkins, were waiting for me. A nice friend had organised it. My Player Profile came alive!

The column

My break into the media was a column in *The Age* newspaper.

I've always been a reader. Mum was a teacher and Dad a librarian. Dad read Roald Dahl novels to me every night before bed. I especially remember *James and the Giant Peach*. If I closed my eyes, I could imagine myself on the peach with James.

My childhood was filled with words and

stories. But it wasn't until *The Age* offered me a column that I wondered if I could be a writer. It was a huge break. I didn't have to go to journalism school like most young writers. Footy sometimes opens amazing doors.

Like with the Player Profile, I didn't want to sound like every other footballer. For team harmony, I couldn't write too much about my teammates or the coach or next week's game. Instead, I wrote about all the other things in a footballer's life — family, cars, social life, movies, friends.

One character who starred in a lot of my columns was Arthur, our sausage dog. Arthur is now 14, and I'm pleased to say he's still going strong.

Stories about Arthur filled my columns.

I wrote about his dislike for wet ground. If it's been raining, Arthur doesn't like to go for a walk.

I wrote about the time I had a bulging disc in my neck, and Arthur also had a sore neck. Weird coincidence? Or dog faking an injury to be like his master?

I wrote about his inability to chase a stick, a ball, anything. Arthur doesn't fetch. Ever.

I wrote about Arthur running in long grass at the park. With his low body, he looked like a canine submarine.

I wrote about our game day routine. First, we'd walk together in tense silence. Then he'd lie on my tummy while I stretched.

Then he'd lie his head on my footy bag while I tried to pack it.

I wrote about the fact that he hates anyone wearing a hi-vis vest!

Arthur, my buddy. My canine love.

He's the character who keeps on giving.

The body of a sausage, but the heart of a Bulldog.

20

In which Bob learns the
brutal nature of fairy tales

Grand Final Day 2016 was the stuff of fairy tales.

It was the Bulldogs' first Grand Final for 55 years. If we won, it'd be our first flag in 62 years.

Every footballer dreams of Grand Finals and premierships.

When I was a little tacker, kicking a ball into the powerlines outside our house in Warragul, I was dreaming of an AFL premiership.

When I walked into Whitten Oval, aged 17, I was dreaming of a premiership.

When I played my first game, I was dreaming of a premiership.

When I was made captain, I was dreaming of one day holding up the cup.

But here's the thing about fairy tales. Sometimes they can be brutal. Especially the old German ones. Do you know that in the original Brothers Grimm 'Cinderella', the stepsisters amputate parts of their feet to try to fit into the slipper? Then there's 'Die Geschichte vom Daumenlutscher'

('The Story of the Thumb-Sucker'). In that one, a mother warns her son not to suck his thumbs. The son ignores her. Then a roving tailor appears and cuts off his thumbs with giant scissors. Whack! Lesson learnt. Don't suck your thumbs.

In 2016, my personal fairy tale also turned a little brutal.

In Round 3, the Bulldogs were on top of the ladder. The team was flying. We were ahead against the reigning premiers, Hawthorn, with 90 seconds to play. My own form was solid. More than solid, even. I'd had 25 possessions or more three weeks in a row. The signs were there. It was the way we were playing. So much daring. So much run. Bevo had us believing. The dream was alive.

Then … I did my knee. It was the same as last time. I heard the crunch of bone and the pop of my ACL.

In an instant, my season was gone. I remember sitting in the rooms afterwards and feeling the grief wash over me. Absolute devastation. We lost the game too. The Hawks kicked the last goal with seconds to go. The full nightmare. I was 34 years old. I felt like I was finished. I was never going to lift that cup.

But the team hung tough. Despite a wretched run with injuries, we made the finals and then strung together a golden September. The boys blitzed the in-form Eagles in Perth, surprising everyone but us. Then we hammered the Hawks and ended their run of three premierships. And in the preliminary final, we won a total thriller against the Giants away in Sydney.

We were in the Grand Final! As the siren sounded, club legend Chris Grant hugged me and whispered, 'We're there.'

I was absolutely over the moon. I'd worried that I might not be, that I'd be too wound up in my own disappointment. But when the moment came, my heart soared. We were there.

On the morning of Grand Final Day, I shuffled around the house. Then I took Arthur for a walk. Then I picked up some coffees from my local café.

I was just killing time.

Finally, I went into the bedroom to get

AFL
AND FINAL

changed into my game day clothes. No, I wasn't playing, but I decided to wear my match day jumper under my club polo shirt anyway.

For luck. And as a symbol.

I wanted to be as close to the players as I possibly could be. With them, supporting them. Wearing the jumper was my way of putting on the war paint.

Just as I lifted my sacred Bulldogs jumper over my head, my wife Justine walked into the room. We stood there together, me in my jumper. A heavy silence filled the room. We both knew there was nothing to say to make things better. Justine started to cry. I cried too.

It was going to be an emotional day.

21

In which the whole world turns
red, white and blue

All week I'd thought we'd win.

I was actually more confident of our chances in the Grand Final against Sydney than I was for any of the other three finals.

We were on a roll. It felt like something historic. It felt like something unstoppable.

In the rooms before the game, it was

surprisingly quiet. Blokes getting changed purposefully. Ankles being taped. Gentle kicking back and forth in the nets.

Outside it was all going on. Pre-match entertainment, a parade of retiring champs. The carnival in full swing.

Inside it all felt like normal.

I felt every emotion. Thrilled that my club was finally playing on Grand Final Day. Nervous about the result. And then there were moments of agony because I would not be playing. It was exhausting, keeping all these emotions in check. I remember hiding in the toilets at one point. I had to present the right face. I was still captain of the club.

The selected 22 had a game to play. The

most important game of their lives.

I was not in the selected 22.

I went from player to player, offering quiet words of support and encouragement. I could tell they were ready to unleash. You get a sense when players are 'on' and when they are 'off'. The mood was fantastic. Every player seemed tuned in to the moment.

Eventually, the players entered the arena. I shared a lift up to level two with Bevo.

Our song blared – 'Sons of the West'! Then the national anthem.

So much noise, so much excitement.

Finally, the opening bounce.

It was a turbo-charged beginning. The Swans had a history of being fast starters and we did well to match them early. Our players showed unbelievable courage. I was sitting in a comfy chair up on level two, writhing with nerves. For most of the first half, my arms were twisted around my body like a pretzel.

Sydney lifted in the second quarter. Their star onballer, Josh Kennedy, was enormous. The Swans led by two points at the break.

In the rooms, our boys were puffed but determined.

The second half was as hard and ferocious as the first. There are moments that will live for all time in Bulldogs history:

Shane Biggs on the forward flank throwing himself into the fray, seven times in one minute. It finished in a goal for Toby McLean.

Easton Wood colliding with Swans playmaker Daniel Hannebery in a brutal hit that injured the Swan's knee.

Jason Johannisen's long bomb from outside 50. On goal review it was called a point.

Dale Morris sneaking up on footy's greatest player, Buddy Franklin, and tackling him from behind.

Tom Boyd picking up the spilled ball and booting the goal that sealed it all.

I couldn't believe it. We'd done it. We were going to win the premiership!

We made our way down to the bench. It was mayhem. Total hysteria. I looked around at all the faces. I'd never witnessed joy like this. My tribe had been waiting decades. The siren sounded, and it was an excuse for us to go bananas some more.

Hugs came from everywhere

Tears flowed.

Everything was red, white and blue.

We'd waited 62 years. And on the 1st of October 2016, it was our turn.

MURPHY'S LORE
IT'S ALL ABOUT
THE
BONT
'BOUT THE BONT

22

In which Bob learns a bit
more about fairy tales

Not many players can say that the greatest moment of their sporting life happened when they weren't playing.

But that's what happened to me.

After the siren, I jumped for joy with everyone else. I'd never seen such happiness. Our 62-year premiership drought was over!

We swarmed onto the MCG.

But my tummy was all jumbled. I couldn't feel the pure joy of the fans, the coaches, the support staff, or the 22 who played. You know that feeling when you're smiling, but there's a tightness in your cheeks?

I kept saying to myself, 'It's not about you, it's not about you.'

But it was hard not to feel some pain on the inside. I'd missed out.

My childhood hero, the great Matthew Richardson, must have seen it in my eyes. Richo stopped me and said, 'I'm feeling for you, Bob.'

After endless hugs, the presentation ceremony began. The knots in my stomach started to ease. My face began to relax. Our supporters were weeping for joy. This really was bigger than any player. Bigger even than the team. This was life-changing for some people. This was history.

The players received their medals. Jason Johannisen won the Norm Smith for best on ground. I was so happy for him.

Then it came time for captain Easton Wood and Bevo. It was less than three years since Luke Beveridge became coach. He had transformed our club. He had shown us a new way. He had welcomed communication between players and coach. I'd never had a relationship like this in footy. Bevo was the reason we'd climbed the mountain.

He was announced to the throng and it

went wild. Bevo was presented with his Jock McHale Medal as coach of the premiership team.

Then he said something amazing. Something that I'd not expected.

'I'd like to call Bob Murphy up to the stand.'

Life would never be the same after hearing that. With just ten words, I was called out of the darkness and into the sunshine. I'd tried to keep the pain to myself, but everyone at the club knew how tough it had been.

Of course I wanted to celebrate my club's greatest triumph.

But of course I also felt some pain about missing out myself.

When Luke called me up to that stage, I felt like I didn't have to pretend anymore.

My teammates hugged the wind out of me. The crowd roared. I floated to the podium. I felt pride. I felt pure joy. But I also felt some sadness. Everything was amplified. Can you imagine? So much colour! So much noise!

I climbed the dais and let out a flood of tears as Easton Wood wrapped his arms around me. What a brilliant captain he'd been. Woody didn't just play a great Grand Final. He'd been the on-field general all year. I felt like a big brother to him. And I was so proud.

Then Bevo said, 'This is yours, mate, you deserve it more than anyone.' He took the

Jock McHale Medal from his own neck and placed it over my head. Then he hugged me. I reckon we all play to make our coach proud. When Bevo hugged me, I felt his love. I felt part of this amazing thing. I was no longer on the outer. I was right in the middle of it all.

The cup arrived on the stage and we were crowned premiers. I grasped one side, Easton held the other. We raised it to the heavens.

The confetti exploded into the air. I'll never forget the noise, the euphoria.

When my knee collapsed, I thought I had said goodbye to a childhood dream. The dream of playing in a premiership. I didn't get to play, but my club had gone all the way, and I could still wear the colours.

So maybe not all fairy tales are brutal and bloody after all.

Maybe some fairy tales are just lovely.

23

In which Bob faces his football death, and survives

I played on in 2017.

On the night my knee went against Hawthorn in 2016, Bevo hugged me in the change rooms. 'Can you come back from this?' he whispered.

I wasn't sure I could. I took a holiday to California with Justine to think it over.

Eventually, I decided that there was a little bit left in the tank. There's a very old and wise saying in football: 'You're a long time retired.'

So I did the rehab. Throughout the Bulldogs' history-making campaign in 2016, I was in the gym, strengthening my knee. On the night that 10,000 fans descended on Whitten Oval in Grand Final week, I was doing my stridethroughs, keeping to the program.

My knee got stronger. I kept my sights on Round 1, 2017.

At times, I didn't think I was going to make it. I retired three times during 2016. But each time I was talked back into giving it a go. Lured by hope.

What if we won the flag in 2017?

What if we went back-to-back?

Hope dragged me back. In Round 1, we beat Collingwood in a great game. I remember sitting on the couch after that game, sore but happy. I'd faced my football death, and survived.

For one more season at least, I was an AFL footballer.

24

In which Bob feels the power,
one last time

Would you allow me to brag for a chapter? If it helps your decision, the chapter after this one is about getting older and knowing when it's time to retire. So it would be nice if I could talk one last time about my glory days. Is that okay with you?

Thanks, I'll be quick.

It was my third-last game of AFL footy. We were playing GWS at Etihad Stadium. Normally when I fill out a form, I write 'half-back flanker' in the spot where it says 'Job/Profession'. But on this day I was up forward.

The Bont won the ball in the middle. His target was Jack Redpath, but straight away I knew he'd over-kicked it. I ran hard, towards the boundary.

The Giants' Harrison Himmelberg was on my hammer. The ball was in front of us both, running away.

Earlier in my football life, I would have backed my leg speed. But now, at age 35, things weren't so simple. I assessed the situation. The boundary line was in front of me, Himmelberg was behind me. I took possession.

Then I did a trick that not everybody knows. I slowed down. It's a weird thing. Sometimes the best way to evade a tackler is to slow down rapidly. And then go fast. It's the change of speed and direction at precisely the same moment that makes someone difficult to tackle. Watch Scott Pendlebury. Or Tom Mitchell. Or the Bont himself. It's kind of like a dance. When you do it right, everything moves in slow motion.

I shifted down a gear and Himmelberg was right on my back. I took possession and shook my hips. Yep, the shimmy! We went left, right, left, all in a split second. I was flat to the floor for speed now.

FIVE LITTLE-KNOWN TRICKS THAT COACHES MIGHT NOT TELL YOU

1. To get away from a tackler, slow down first and then go as fast as you can while turning at the exact same moment. You'll lose them!

2. When you kick a banana shot at goal, aim higher than you normally would.

3. Watch your opponents' eyes when he kicks the ball. That's where it's going.

4. Practise snap kicks on your opposite foot. They'll get you out of trouble on the field.

5. Throw some grass up. See what the wind is doing!

He lunged, tried to grip, but I was able to wriggle free. I turned for the pocket. Over my left shoulder I glimpsed the goal. Things felt right. The rhythm of the play. The rhythm of my legs. My last thought was 'balance'.

I held the ball softly and swung my leg through. I tried not to kick it too hard. The contact was sweet. That feeling a cricketer has when the ball hits the exact middle of the bat.

I knew it was a goal as the ball left my boot. It's the most exhilarating feeling I've ever known. A clean, crisp, musical note. It might never feel this perfect again.

The ball spun and arced through the middle. People rose to their feet. I surged towards the fence and it was a sea of red, white and blue. The clan. My clan. They felt what I felt.

I pumped my fists back and forth, from them to me and back again. I wanted them to know I felt the connection too.

I wanted to savour this sport I've loved, this sport that has loved me back.

One last time.

25

In which Bob takes a trip to
Mars, and doesn't much like it

I'd like to tell you about the time I went to
Mars. Yep, Mars Stadium, Ballarat, named
after the chocolate bar.

We were playing Port Adelaide in the
town of my birth, Ballarat. And after a
mixed season, the Bulldogs needed to win
to stay in the race for the finals.

Ballarat is a little over an hour north of Melbourne, and is famous for being a bit cold in August.

But I wasn't too worried. Yes, I'd left Ballarat when I was two, but I was still pretty much a local. Surely the cold wouldn't affect me.

Yoooooooooooooow!

That was the sound I made stepping out of the car.

Sheeeeeeeeeeeesh!

That's the sound I made walking the oval the night before the game.

I looked at the sky. Surely a drift of snow had to go with cold like this.

I had a sore throat. Blocked sinuses. But I was always going to play. Professional footballers put up with injury and illness all the time.

Remember those beautiful words in Mike Brady's 'Up There Cazaly'?

There are days when you could give it up

There are days when you could fly

That day at Mars Stadium, I didn't feel like flying.

I struggled from the outset to find my spark. My legs felt heavy. I couldn't get into my stride.

At one point I grabbed the ball, and thought I might kick a goal, but Port's Tom Jonas buried me in the tackle.

I was surprised he got me.

He drove me into the grass as he got back up.

I tried to be tough. I slapped the back of his head and said some mean things. Almost immediately, I regretted my flash of anger and wondered who I was becoming. I've never been the 'tough guy' type. I've always let my footy do the talking.

I had a shot at goal in the second quarter which would have given us a very handy lead. I struck it well, but it drifted just a little and slammed into the post.

The Port players offered me some goal-kicking advice.

I lost my temper again. Said some more mean things. Who was this version of me? I was turning into a grumpy old man.

It was a scrappy game in the second half. Neither side could shrug the other. Kicking

goals was tricky in the freezing winds of Ballarat.

Late in the game, I handballed to Luke Dahlhaus and Port's Brett Ebert collected me with a massive hip and shoulder.

We clashed heads. A little cut opened under my right eye. I stayed down. The doctors arrived. 'Body or head?' they asked.

'Everything,' I said.

There are days when you could give it up
There are days when you could fly

The problem with getting older is that there are fewer days when you could fly.

And more days when you could give it up.

We lost the game on Mars (Stadium). It was close all day, but Port got hold of us in the last few minutes.

The loss meant that the Bulldogs almost certainly wouldn't make the finals in 2017.

I'd decided not to continue in 2018.

Therefore, I would never play in a premiership.

I'd always have that hole in my heart as a footballer.

I drove away from Ballarat that night with tears rolling down my face.

Footy can be tough some days. Even for those of us lucky enough to live the dream.

26

In which Bob the footballer
says goodbye

The 14th of August 2017.

I retired on the same day as Luke Hodge.

At least I thought I did.

Hodgey's retirement lasted about five minutes, until he was back out there, but as a Lion instead of a Hawk.

Luke Hodge might be the best leader I

ever saw. And one of the best players too. When he played in defence, he never stopped talking. He'd tell his teammates where to stand. 'One metre to your left, Strats.' 'Get boundary side, Birch.' He had an amazing reaction time and a sense of where the ball would land.

I told you I loved life on the flanks.

Hodgey brought a simple beauty to life on the flanks.

For my 312th and last game, I went into the trainers' room and stuck some Vicks up my nose. Just like I had for the previous 311. For me, eucalyptus gel was like war paint. Once the Vicks went up the snozzer, I was ready for action.

MY FIVE FAVOURITE OPPONENTS

1. Cyril Rioli – It was scary playing
   against Cyril. Not just because he
   could literally do anything with the
   ball. I got scared even when I had the
   ball! He was such a fierce chaser and
   tackler you never knew when he was
   coming. It was like knowing there was
   a shark out there in the water with
   you. Was Cyril coming? Oh no, he's
   coming, isn't he? Nooooooooo!

2. Steve Johnson – Stevie J is one of
   the greats of Geelong's greatest era.
   He was also extremely cheeky and
   talkative. One day, he did a sneaky
   interchange and ran straight from
   the bench to the goal square. After
   kicking a goal while his opponent (me!)
   was stranded somewhere near the
   centre square, he ran back and said,
   'Did you see me come on the ground?
   It was quite rascalish, wasn't it?'

3. Richo — I watched him kick ten goals one day, and wanted to cheer, but it was against my Bulldogs!

4. Wayne Campbell — I grew up with his number on my back and one day we were playing on each other. The ball got kicked out in front of us, and Wayne whispered out the side of his mouth, 'It's a foot race.' I almost stumbled because I laughed. You're not meant to laugh on a footy field.

5. The Cornes brothers, Chad and Kane — Neither of them were likeable on the field. Cocky, brash and terrific posture. Off the field, I really like them. That's a bit annoying and a bit of a life lesson.

It's a special feeling right before the game. You're kind of on edge. You know that very soon the siren will sound and it will be on. You know you have a job to do, and you feel the weight of the pressure you put on yourself to play well.

But you're also with your teammates. You're part of a gang. There's a sense of brotherhood.

On that last night, the change rooms were quiet. I could hear the frenzied noise just beyond the concrete walls. Time inched forward. The little time I had left.

I dipped my hands in resin. It's a kind of sticky glue that players use on their hands. When you apply resin and slap a footy from hand to hand, it feels like you will mark anything! Again, it's a thing I'd done 311 times before.

All these rituals.

All those games.

Bevo gave us our final instructions. Did we listen to his actual words? It's more about a mood and a feel than anything else. We broke from the circle and headed for the door. The noise grew louder.

Behind me were our boys, my boys. I had felt such pride and privilege being captain of this team.

We all strode purposefully forward, ascending together. In a few moments, we'd burst onto the arena. I walked slowly, savouring this feeling for the last time.

It was my favourite feeling, the one just before the contest. When the excitement and the anticipation reach fever pitch.

When it is all in front of you.

On Friday 25th of August 2017, we ran onto the ground, lifted by our fans and our song. 'Sons of the West, red, white and blue'. I was floating, soaring.

I was living my childhood dream, as I had been for my whole adult life.

And I was going to savour it, one last time.

27

In which Bob looks at his
ugly knees and thinks
about dreams

Justine and I have three kids.

They are Jarvis (now eleven), Frankie (nine) and Delilah (five). They all have crooked little fingers, just like me. They also have my eyes. Other than that, they look a lot like their mum. Given that I think she's the most beautiful person alive, that's okay by me.

A few months after I played my last game, we went on a family holiday to Byron Bay. It's such a lovely place. The sand is white and soft. The sun rises over perfect rows of rolling sea foam, and sets behind luscious green hinterland. Often, you'll spot a dolphin leaping or a whale breaching. Beaches don't come much better than Byron.

One evening, Justine and I watched our kids splashing in the shallows. I could feel the still-warm sand through my damp swimming shorts. I looked at my skinny knees lined with scars. Ugly knees, now. Footy demands you pay a price. Every player who is lucky enough to have a lengthy career finishes with battle scars and pains.

I watched my kids and thought about how lucky I was.

Lucky to have Justine.

Lucky to have three healthy and (mostly) happy kids.

Lucky to have been a professional footballer for my entire adult life.

Lucky to have lived THE dream. The only one I ever had. The dream of being an AFL footballer.

I've talked a bit about dreams in this book. Not the sleepy-time ones, although I could tell you about the time I dreamt that the moon was inhabited by an evil goat, who drove a ute, and caused destruction by shooting laser beams at Earth.

But I'm talking about life-goal dreams.

I'm talking about ambition and hope.

I'm talking about that distant, hazy figure in your mind that is a grown-up you. What do you see that person doing? What would be the best-case scenario?

Sometimes your dream seems so silly you don't even want to say it out loud.

What if I could be prime minister? What if I could be an actor in movies? What if I started a successful company? What if I invented something that changed the world? What if I painted something that was hung in a major gallery? What if I helped the hungry and the homeless?

What if I went to the Olympics? What if I played AFL or AFLW?

I don't think Jarvis, Frankie or Delilah share my footy dream. That's fine by me. If they are lucky enough to sit on a beach at Byron Bay when they are 35, I'm guessing they'll have much prettier knees.

But I do hope they have their own dreams. In fact, I know they do. And when life pushes them one way or another, like the Byron Bay waves, I hope their dreams bend towards the happiest possible future.

I hope you are dreaming too.

Because dreams sustain us. They give our lives focus, and push us along in the things we love doing.

There was once a boy called Bob, who

came from Warragul, who kicked a footy into powerlines every night, and who ended up playing in the big league.

Real life wasn't quite the same as the dream, but it was pretty darn close.

And it was brilliant.

Bob Murphy played for the Western Bulldogs for 17 years and was their captain from 2015 to 2017. In 2015 Murphy was named captain of the year at the AFL Players Association awards and was also captain of the All-Australian team. The following year, the Bulldogs won their first premiership in 62 years. He is the author of two books for adults, *Murphy's Lore* and *Leather Soul*.

Tony Wilson is a much-loved Australian author. His books for children include *The Princess and the Packet of Frozen Peas*, *The Cow Tripped Over the Moon*, *Hickory Dickory Dash* and *The Selwood Boys*. He's also a one-time Hawthorn draftee, but unlike Bob, Tony never played a single AFL game. Sob! He loves a great footy story, though, and enjoyed helping Bob share his. Tony and his wife Tamsin have four children and live in Melbourne. Coincidentally, they attend the same primary school as Bob's kids.

www.ingramcontent.com/pod-product-compliance
Lightning Source LLC
Chambersburg PA
CBHW022141050726
47590CB00002B/526